the little book of
MANIFESTING

Hardie Grant

QUADRILLE

Manifest

Definition:

verb

- Showing or embodying something abstract or theoretical.

- The action or fact of showing something.

- Making everything you want to think and feel a reality... via your thoughts, actions, beliefs and emotions; allowing and trusting that the universe will bring all you desire and wish.

Manifesting means. . .

Asking the universe

Being purposeful

Curating your own future

Daring to dream

Manifesting makes you the captain of your ship of life. You may come up against storms, sea monsters, dangerous currents and hostile pirates, but as the captain of your ship, you will plan to safely navigate the journey. And, like all good captains, you will summon help from the crew, technology and the elements. You will gather the power of the wind and follow the course of the stars to seek a safe harbour at a destination of your choosing.

How to manifest a successful life voyage

- Visualize your destination
- Seek investment in your journey
- Chart your course
- Choose your shipmates
- Anticipate storms
- Harness the power of the elements
- Adjust your sails when buffeted
- Keep a steady course
- Land safely

The five golden principles of manifesting

1. Be clear about what you desire.

2. Ask the cosmos for help.

3. Trust your desires to align with what will benefit you. If your desire does not manifest immediately, have faith that it will appear when the stars align.

4. Take action to support your journey.

5. Practise gratitude for all that pulls you closer to what you desire.

Manifesting has been practised since the very first moment that humans gazed up at the heavens, closed their eyes and wished upon a star. The *Chandogya Upanishad,* one of the oldest Vedic sacred writings, proves that manifesting is a concept with at least 8,000 years of history.

"From it the universe comes forth, in it the universe merges and in it the universe breathes. Therefore a man should meditate on Brahman [the supreme existence] with a calm mind. Now, verily, a man consists of will. As he wills in this world, so does he become when he has departed hence. Let him with this knowledge in mind form his wit."

Chandogya Upanishad

"Star light, star bright,
First star I see tonight.
I wish I may, I wish I might,
Have the wish I wish tonight."

ANONYMOUS

Harness the power of the present tense

Develop the habit of using the present tense when unpacking what you desire.

Using strong, affirmative language helps impress upon your subconscious that what you desire is already part of you. Rather than saying, 'I will be a decisive and compassionate leader', say instead, 'I *am* a decisive and compassionate leader'. And for things a little further out of reach, swap, 'I will be a millionaire' for 'I am in control of my flourishing finances'.

"*All things are in the universe, and the universe is in all things: we in it, and it in us; in this way everything concurs in a perfect unity.*"

GIORDANO BRUNO

Fancy manifesting a new apartment into existence?

Simples. Write down: 'A new apartment. A new apartment. A new apartment', close your eyes and cross your fingers. Hey presto! You've manifested it and will collect the keys on Monday. What could go wrong?

The art of manifesting, however, is not magic. Spells are not required. If only life (and mortgage applications) were that simple. Manifesting is instead the art of turning an intention into a reality.

So, you would like a new apartment. Hold that thought, write it down, turn it over in your mind, let it swell within you, see it in black and white, reread it, share your words with others. The art of manifesting begins here, settles into the intention and articulates the desire.

Much like our online shopping 'basket', the act of manifesting requires us to imagine the object of our desire in our mind's eye, as if it is already ours. It sits, waiting for us to click 'check out'.

Visualize your mind's basket containing the perfect necklace for your sister's significant birthday, for example. While the online purchase takes one click, the transfer of the object from our mind's basket to checkout requires input from ourselves, others and the cosmos.

Picturing the ideal necklace as if
it is already yours will help you to
recognize it in a shop window when
you least expect it.

"Give, and it shall be given unto you."

Luke 6:38

Successful manifesting can be found in those who model the behaviours and gifts that they are seeking. Whether we understand this as divine grace or as karma, this virtuous circle lies at the heart of what it means to manifest.

To receive love, love.

To receive kindness, be kind.

To receive riches, be generous.

Affirmations to promote *giving* in order to receive

Copy these into your journal or write them as notes that you may wish to place beneath your pillow, or carry close to your heart. By embracing the behaviours you desire, you are more likely to attract similar behaviours in return.

I am generous and I am worthy of generosity.

I share my goodwill with others and receive the goodwill of others.

I am kind and compassionate and worthy of both.

I treat people with respect and I receive respect.

I am trustworthy and honest and worthy of honesty in return.

It helps to be honest about the motivation behind our manifesting intention. If it is to impress others, to achieve public applause or online recognition, question whether this is the ideal path. In all things, seek personal growth for its own sake, in a way that truly serves you and others.

Never settle for being an extra. Be the star in your own life.

Sometimes, manifesting our desires can seem vague and difficult to articulate. Ask yourself probing questions to give form to swirling, out-of-reach wishes. Ask yourself:

What would I love to. . .

Tell my family?

Hold soon?

Feel every day?

Where would I love to. . .

Spend my money?

Call home?

Take my loved one?

Who would I love to. . .

Call my own?

Wake up next to?

Always rely on?

When would I love to...

Be financially free?

Feel peace?

Accept love?

When beginning the process of manifesting, it helps to ask yourself open-hearted questions. After asking, give the question room to settle, and prepare space within yourself for answers to present themselves.

Open-hearted question prompts

If I were to *not* fail, what would I want to do?

How have I changed in the past five years?

When did I last feel pure joy?

Questions to ask before manifesting

1. Will this really make me happy and fulfilled?

2. Am I prepared to deal with the consequences if I am successful?

3. Will anyone be harmed by my manifesting?

Be your own manifesting model

Much is made in parenting manuals about 'modelling' good behaviour, rather than simply 'telling' children how to behave. This idea aligns with the principle of manifestation. If you are asking the universe for a 'better working relationship with your junior', model their desired behaviour. If you are seeking more income streams, model financial acuity: read financial journals and research investment strategies. If you are seeking a best friend, model healthy friendship attributes: arrange social events, check in and initiate conversations.

Carry your manifesting intentions with you

Locket: write your intention on a tiny piece of paper. Scroll the paper within a locket.

Phone: write down your intention, then place between your phone and case.

Clothes: embroider your intention on your favourite shirt or jacket, close to your heart.

Braid: weave meaningful colours into hair braids – yellow for positivity, red for love, gold for wealth. Repeat your intention as you braid.

Anoint yourself with oil before you begin your manifesting ritual

Add a tiny dab at each ear to open up your listening heart.

A tiny dab between your eyes will open your mind's eye.

Manifesting allows you to step into the image you have created of yourself.

So you want to become fit, create an image of yourself as already fit:

I am a runner.

Visualize yourself running through your favourite landscape, feel the wind in your face, feel the ground beneath your feet, feel the exhilaration as you shower afterwards, the refreshing water on hot skin. See the clothes you will wear, plan the routes you will take.

Create an image of yourself as a runner and step into that image. On the days when you haven't managed to run, say to yourself: 'Fear not, for I am a runner'. Tomorrow is another opportunity to step into the image of yourself that already exists.

If you prefer writing to speaking and feel happiest curled up with a book, you may respond more naturally and fully to manifesting intentions that are articulated in writing, rather than those spoken aloud.

For those of who prefer to read and write, there are endless methods for manifesting, from the penning of short, snappy mantras, to the lengthy 'scripting' device, where you treat your intentions as a playwright would care for her leading character.

Make your affirmations and intentions word-perfect

There is immense power in the copying and repetition of words. Anyone who has learned a poem by heart or can recall their single line from the school play, understands how deeply embedded in our minds words become. Words filter through our psyche and reside in our memory to be called upon when required. It is therefore desirable to think deeply and deliberately about each and every word of our affirmations and intentions.

"I know nothing in the world has as much power as a word. Sometimes I write one, and I look at it, until it begins to shine."

EMILY DICKINSON

"Life must not be a novel that is given to us, but one that is made by us."

NOVALIS

Seven steps to writing a word-perfect intention

1. **Mull.** Imagine you would like to manifest a holiday with your sister. Let the idea settle and encourage your imagination to luxuriate in all options. A city break? A beach holiday? Home? Abroad? Let inspiration spirit you away to myriad places.

2. **Distil.** Once your desired holiday has come into focus, sit with the image and visualize you and your sister at its heart.

3. **Clarify.** Focus in on the details. What can you see? How is the weather? What are you drinking?

What are you both saying to each other? What colour is the sky?

4. **Draft.** Experiment with articulating the holiday you wish to share with your sister. I am taking my sister on holiday to Barbados. My sister and I are holidaying together in Ibiza. I am relaxed in a spa with my sister. Carefully consider each and every word until you are happy that your sentence perfectly summarizes your holiday intention.

5. **Write.** Once you have carefully crafted your manifesting intention, copy it beautifully using your favourite pen and paper. My sister and I are spending a long weekend together swimming in the warm waters of the Adriatic.

6. **Memorize.** Learn each word off by heart, roll them around in your mouth until you taste their power.

7. **Recognize the manifesting.** The holiday will appear for you, either in the pages of a magazine, the window of a travel agent or during an online scroll. You will recognize it as already yours and make the appropriate arrangements.

"*In this state of absorbed contemplation, there is no longer any question of holding an object in view; the vision is such that seeing and seen are one; object and act of vision become identical.*"

PLOTINUS

Kickstart intense manifesting using the 5x55 method

Like Victorian schooling, the 5x55 manifesting method works on the premise that the repetition of writing lines will impress upon the subconscious and the cosmos the necessity of your words.

1. Carefully craft your affirmation to make every word count.

2. Choose a time you can spend manifesting every day for five days.

3. Copy your manifestation affirmation 55 times over five consecutive days.

When writing your manifesting intention, trust in the depths of your soul to speak to you. Take up a pen and begin to write your thoughts and desires. First one word, then another if you allow yourself, and soon, the whole page will be covered.

"Thought engenders thought. Place one idea on paper, another will follow it, and still another, until you have written a page; you cannot fathom your mind. There is a well of thought which has no bottom; the more you draw from it, the more clear and fruitful it will be."

GEORGE AUGUSTUS SALA

Manifesting as scriptwriting

- Imagine you are a scriptwriter, sketching out your next film where you are the star of your own movie.

- Alight on the movie's concept: action, romance, drama, historical epic, gritty urban thriller?

- Establish the movie's location: beach, city, countryside, exotic destination?

- Create a narrative arc whereby the star (AKA you) overcome various obstacles before achieving success and happiness with the partner of their choice.

- Write a 'call sheet': when will filming begin, who are the supporting roles, what props are needed for success?

- Write character descriptions for the casting director: what clothes will the star wear, how is their hair, what look are they channelling?

- When will the wrap party take place?

Eight manifesting journaling prompts

1. I am dedicating myself to self-growth by...

2. My income streams are flowing richly by...

3. This year I am accomplishing...

4. Today I am choosing to...

5. Success at work looks like...

6. My friendship is being deepened by...

7. In my heart, I know I am responsible for my own...

8. This, I will release from my past...

Use different journals for different aspects of manifesting

Investing in separate journals when manifesting love, business, self-development, friendships and finances will help keep your mind uncluttered and your vibration levels open. Imagine four separate roads out of town, rather than a single, traffic-filled underpass.

Easy 369 method

Write down your manifesting desire:
three times in the morning.

Repeat your manifesting desire:
six times in the afternoon.

Write down your manifesting desire:
nine times in the evening.

Five ideas for manifesting if you are an auditory learner

1. Hash out your manifesting ideas with a friend: talk, talk, talk until your intention has made itself clear.

2. Find an app that will play affirmations/intentions/guided meditations to you as you exercise.

3. Use soft, gentle music as you meditate your manifestations to prevent distraction.

4. Read aloud your manifesting desires and listen to the shape of your words, emphasizing the most important.

5. Auditory learners are great communicators: tell others of your manifesting desires and use your magnificent powers of persuasion to bear on the universe.

For kinaesthetic learners, a hands-on approach to manifesting may be called for. If you are sensitive to texture and feeling, choose manifesting methods that arouse all five senses.

- If manifesting a new business, imagine the feeling of your new premises, picture yourself handling the items you are selling, envisage the smell of your office stationery.

- Act as if the manifesting has already occurred. Visit suitable office venues, create an identity for your business, print and distribute business cards.

- Speak your manifestation to your favourite crystal and keep it about your person.

Three tactile manifesting ideas

1. Plant spring bulbs in autumn.
    Repeat your manifestation intention
    as you tenderly bury the bulbs
    in the nourishing soil. Work to
    nature's timetable and watch as
    your manifestations flower when the
    bulbs unfurl their petals.

2. Make a batch of jam or pickle
    and whisper your intention into
    the bubbling pan. Create pretty
    labels: 'My Positivity Chutney',
    or 'Dreams of Romance Hedgerow
    Jam' and distribute to friends
    and neighbours.

3. Assemble a necklace for manifesting. Invest in a chain and adorn with meaningful objects, such as your mother's ring, your aunt's charm. Speak your intention to each item as you thread it through the chain. Allow yourself to repeat your intention whenever you choose to wear the necklace, and remind yourself of what you long for every time you touch it.

Don't be afraid to let all your senses absorb your manifesting intention.

If you wish to become a novelist, familiarize yourself with the object of your desire. Choose your favourite book and close your eyes. Feel the pages beneath your fingers, take in the smell as you flick through the pages, listen to the pages as they move beneath your hands.

Hold the book close to your heart and speak your intention, 'I am a published novelist' into its spine.

Return the book to the shelf knowing that your story is already being heard.

Inspired by a passage in 1 Kings where God speaks to Elijah not through fire or wind or great spectacle, but through the 'still small voice', this idea of being guided, if we listen carefully enough, has gently taken hold of the human heart. Some call the 'still small voice' God, others, conscience, others, the universe. But everyone agrees that the 'still small voice' can be heard if we are willing to listen. With manifesting, the 'still small voice' can help direct your desires to clear paths and towards goals that will ultimately benefit you.

Five ways to tune into your 'still small voice'

1. Place yourself beside water, watch and listen.

2. Create a comfort zone in your home where you sit in peace.

3. Walk somewhere beautiful, alone and without electronic devices.

4. If gripped with panic and fear, do not listen to the clamouring noisy voices; wait for quiet to return and then hear.

5. Because you have opened yourself to the 'still small voice', when answers do manifest, they will slot easily into the space you have made for them.

"How many things [. . .] are looked upon as quite impossible until they have been actually effected?"

PLINY THE ELDER

Using a manifesting vision board

Online or offline, the vision board speaks powerfully to those who respond to visual cues. Sumptuous colours, big, bold graphics, words that speak to your heart. Created from magazine images, old photographs, hand-written quotes, pressed flowers, restaurant receipts and other personal, visual items, the vision board is a powerful tool in the manifester's armoury. It must be striking enough to stop you in your tracks and remind you of your goals, and inspiring enough for you to fully appreciate that these goals are within your grasp.

Visualize your manifesting intention
with your mind's eye.

Mind's eye

Definition:

noun

The mental faculty of conceiving an imaginary or recollected scene.

"Don't be pushed by your problems, be led by your dreams."

RALPH WALDO EMERSON

How to prepare to create a manifesting vision board

1. Spend a period of time concentrating/meditating/recalling exactly what you wish to manifest. Let your desires permeate your being before you begin.

2. Create your vision board in a place of comfort and beauty. Light candles, play uplifting music, revel in the activity.

3. Keep your goal specific. If you are working towards personal development goals, focus on one word or idea, 'confidence' for example, and build your vision on its foundation.

Manifesting is. . .

Making decisions

Resolve

A self-fulfilling prophecy

Starting with a dream

Visualization

Manifesting idea: create a vision board of the very best you

Rather than selecting images of glossy Hollywood influencers, choose your most beloved images of yourself from childhood to this morning. Find images where your smile is at its most vivacious, your happiness most abundant and your ease most graceful. Only then look at your hair and your clothes to see which styles and pieces you wish to elevate and update. Let yourself absorb the feeling that these images of the very best you are a reminder of who you truly are. Manifest these combined images of yourself and step into that feeling.

Three steps for the perfect manifesting vision board

1. Dedicate a decent amount of time to this project: your dreams are worth a good few hours of careful curation.

2. Respect your manifesting desires by treating them to the finest vision-board materials your budget can stretch to.

3. Whether working on a cork board or online, tenderly cut out images, graphics and words. Treat each image with care. The ritual of creating the board will further help absorb your manifesting goals to your subconscious.

How to use your manifesting vision board

1. Display your board where it will have the most impact. Allocate a space where you will be happy to contemplate your vision. It ought to be a focal point for contemplation, not a distraction.

2. Dedicate a few moments of each day to sitting with your manifesting vision board and meditating on what the images mean to you.

3. Photograph the board on your phone and refer to it whenever you need a course correction or a positive energy boost.

Get gluing!

Beware the reproachful manifesting vision board!

Keep your mood boards precious to you and avoid populating with entirely unobtainable images. If you are working on improving your fitness and energy levels, consider the wisdom of filling your mood board with the sleekest of Hollywood stars whose entire working life is dedicated to the body beautiful. Instead, select images and inspiration closer to home: a friend who has achieved a healthier lifestyle, an image of yourself brimming with energy, a new pair of training shoes. Once you have achieved your smaller goals then by all means create ever more glamorous mood boards.

Three ways to manifest love

1. Keep one drawer empty – you are literally making space for your lover to fill when your stars align.

2. Script the hero/heroine of the romantic novel of your life. What do they love? How do they make you feel? How do you look as a pair?

3. Visualize yourself being introduced to your lover; fill the scene with details. Where are you? What are you both wearing? Is it a party? A fitness group? How does their hand feel in yours? When opportunities arise to attend similar venues – say yes!

Sensory tip when manifesting love

It is love that most expands our senses, therefore you should manifest love when your senses are most aroused. Consider when in the day you feel most invigorated, when the joy of life is pulsing. For some this will be during a run or wild swimming, for others as they lie sweating in a sauna or curled up with a hot chocolate. Whenever your senses are fully alive, choose this moment to contemplate love. Tune yourself into your aroused body and contemplate who you would like to share this feeling with. Let your senses lead you and allow your body to respond when the image of your lover materializes.

How to compile a manifesting love board

Love is about so much more than a three-word dating bio or a sketched image of the 'ideal lover'. Love is intense feeling, it is serene security, it is exhilarating pleasure and peaceful joy. Rather than fixating on what your lover will look like or do for a living, concentrate on the feelings they will engender in you.

Ask yourself which romantic scenes in films have moved you (that scene in *The English Patient*), which love poetry has made you cry (anything by Pablo Neruda), which painters have captured true love (Klimt's 'The Kiss' of course!) and which novels depict the joy of lifelong partnership (*P.S. I Love You* by Cecelia Ahern). Create the most romantic of mood boards of poetry, great art, film posters and novel extracts. Plunder the feelings of love that others have so brilliantly captured and make them your own. Once you have bathed in the depictions of true love, you will be well placed to recognize those feelings when they inevitably strike you.

Three executive tips when manifesting financial security

1. Ask yourself when in the day you feel most competent. Are you a lark or an owl? When do you best whizz through your to-do list? Choose this time to attempt financial manifesting – when your technical, competent brain is firing.

2. Consider what you wear and the place you choose to manifest in. Manifesting in a smart outfit, at a desk, will help you step into the right financial frame of mind.

3. Consider all the details. If you are journaling your manifestations for financial success, is the pink fluffy journal really appropriate? What materials would a super-smart business person use?

Three ways to clear financial blockages

1. Sort out your wallet/phone. Remove cards that are no longer needed (yes, all of them!).

2. Include an intention card in your newly cleansed purse. 'I am financially astute and my use of this wallet shall bring me wealth, not debt.'

3. Be brave and fully grasp your online accounts/debt. See the real figures and process them. Call in professional help where necessary.

Reframe your limiting beliefs

'But I'm not from a wealthy family'
… 'I'm in a low-paid job'… 'I have too
many dependents'…

While we all have limiting elements
to our lives, it is possible to turn these
into positive affirmations.

'I am the first in my family to be
financially secure'… 'My low-paid job
is the first step to a high-paid job'…
'I am grateful for my dependents and
I model financially astute behaviours
for them.'

Five positive money affirmations

I attract all the true riches of life.

I am in charge of my money, my money is not in charge of me.

I am worthy of wealth.

My financial fortune brings fortune to others.

I am surrounded by financial opportunity.

" *The stars are like letters that inscribe themselves at every moment in the sky. Everything in the world is full of signs. All events are coordinated. All things depend on each other. Everything breathes together.*"

PLOTINUS

Remember the cosmos before the 18th-century Enlightenment, when planets had characters – warlike Mars and gentle Venus – and cast their gravity on human affairs. The night sky sparkled with constellations of heroes and heroines – Orion, the Seven Sisters, Pegasus – and humans existed in communion with a lively cosmos. Now in this age of science, the silent universe is known simply as space.

Manifesting invites us to return to ancient ideas of an active cosmos, where we are participants in an ordered, not accidental universe, and the powers of the sun, the planets and the stars have the potential to combine with our own efforts for human fulfilment.

Light travels around the universe at 186,000 miles per second – the universe loves speed and is quite happy to work at pace.

The ABC of speedy manifesting

Act on your desire from the moment you have shared it with the universe.

Believe that your desire has already been fulfilled.

Clarity of vision: keep your desire measurable and time-limited.

Believe in the power of vibration to explain the success of manifesting

A few centuries from now, the science of vibration will be as easily explained as gravity and other such truths that once baffled mankind. For now, quantum vibration is vastly complicated, involving fiendish maths such as Schrödinger's Equation, which demonstrates how all matter vibrates.

Let us simply accept the basic principle that the entire cosmos vibrates, all matter is energy and there are universe-wide oceans of energy available for us to tap into and vibrate our way to success.

"Quantum physics thus reveals the basic oneness of the universe."

ERWIN SCHRÖDINGER

" *We must not wait for things to come, believing that they are decided by irrescindable destiny. If we want it, we must do something about it.*"

ERWIN SCHRÖDINGER

"As a man who has devoted his whole life to the most clear-headed science, to the study of matter, I can tell you as a result of my research about atoms this much: There is no matter as such. All matter originates and exists only by virtue of a force which brings the particle of an atom to vibration and holds this most minute solar system of the atom together."

MAX PLANCK

Ten ways to improve high vibrations

Smile

Be kind to everyone you meet

Show gratitude

Practise forgiveness

Compliment, don't complain

Find the good

Notice beauty

Be generous

Be present

Love with abundance

*"The individual soul should seek
for an intimate union with the soul
of the universe."*

NOVALIS

If you are asking the universe for help... respond universally

So you've asked the universe for help in finding a new job. You have followed your favourite manifesting methods and your 'new job' is firmly lodged in your subconscious.

Let this desire become manifest universally.

Dress for your new job. Share your desire with your social network, on and offline. Reach out to companies.

Practise introducing yourself with your new job title. Keep dressing for your new job. Rehearse what you will say to your new team on your first day. Let your desire permeate your being universally. When the new job arrives you effortlessly slide into it, as it is already yours.

Rediscover the Anima Mundi

Manifesting rests on the idea that the universe is animate, alive and we exist in communion with it. This knowledge was held true by the ancients who understood that the world has a soul known as the Anima Mundi. Plato wrote over 2,400 years ago: 'The cosmos is a single Living Creature which contains all living creatures within it.' Use this concept to reimagine reality so we are living within a soulful world and can act in harmony with it, to both give and receive.

Three ways to reconnect with the Anima Mundi, the soul of the world

1. Recognize life in the world wherever you walk: the cracks in the pavement teeming with insects, the urban tree that's home to a thousand leaves.

2. Express gratitude to the ground beneath your feet. It is firm and holds you steady as you move around its surface.

3. Look into the heart of a flower, see its minute filaments and recognize its beauty.

Becoming more in tune with the Anima Mundi will help the practice of manifesting. Rather than shouting into the universe's silent abyss, speaking from your soul to the soul of the world will be a far more intimate experience.

> *"Nothing is stronger than thought for it travels over the universe, and nothing is stronger than necessity because all must submit to it."*

THALES

The most perfect example of the power of manifesting is revealed in the children's story *The Gruffalo*. Written by Julia Donaldson, *The Gruffalo* tells of a mouse frightening off predators by telling them of his friend the Gruffalo, a monster with 'terrible tusks and terrible claws and terrible teeth in his terrible jaws.' And lo, as soon as the mouse has escaped all his predators, the terrible Gruffalo appears!

The idea that what exists in your head must also exist in the world has firm theological foundations and can be traced back to the 11th century, when St Anselm suggested the ontological argument for the existence of God: essentially that that which exists in the mind must also exist in reality.

"The thing you set your mind on is the thing you ultimately become."

NATHANIEL HAWTHORNE

Quantum physics tells us that energy can't be destroyed – it can only change in form. Therefore the positive energy you send out into the cosmos will continue to swirl around as positive energy forever. And one day, it will circle back to you in a changed but still positive form.

Be your radiant self. Radiate your positive thoughts and energy to all you meet. Share your radiance with all you smile to. Give your radiance to those who care for you.

Meet Charles F. Haanel, one of the earliest modern writers to articulate ideas of manifesting. *The Master Key System*, published in 1916, was groundbreaking and elaborates on ways to concentrate on one's desires, visualize one's success and appreciate one's unity with God.

" The predominant thought or the mental attitude is the magnet, and the law is that 'like attracts like', consequently, the mental attitude will invariably attract such conditions as correspond to its nature."

CHARLES F. HAANEL

"Whatever you desire for yourself, affirm it for others, and it will help you both. We reap what we sow. If we send out thoughts of love and health, they return to us like bread cast upon the waters; but if we send out thoughts of fear, worry, jealousy, anger, hate, etc., we will reap the results in our own lives."

CHARLES F. HAANEL

The 'law of attraction' method recognizes the power our emotions have on ourselves and others. In its simplest form, this means: be positive and you will create positivity. Be negative, create negativity.

We've all noticed how the attraction method works. We've seen the cheerful person who spreads joy. We've seen the opposite, a doom-laden misery who drags down everyone's energy levels. We all need to observe ourselves and ask, who are we?

Do we want positive or negative energy and outcomes? It's our choice.

*"You create your own universe
as you go along."*

WINSTON CHURCHILL

The 12 Universal Laws offer a spiritual foundation for manifesting, resting on the idea of the inter-connectedness of the cosmos and the eternal interchange of energy.

The Law of Oneness: Everything is connected.

The Law of Vibration: Everything is in constant motion and vibrates at certain frequencies.

The Law of Action: Success requires action.

The Law of Correspondence: The external world is determined by our internal world.

The Law of Cause and Effect: All actions have reactions.

The Law of Compensation: Your efforts will never go unnoticed.

The Law of Attraction: Your energy will attract what you desire.

The Law of Perpetual Transmission of Energy: Your energy will continue throughout the cosmos.

The Law of Relativity: Your reality is based on your perception.

The Law of Polarity: Everything has a polar opposite.

The Law of Rhythm: There is a natural cycle to everything.

The Law of Gender: We are made up of masculine and feminine energy.

" *When you say to yourself, 'I am going to have a pleasant visit or a pleasant journey,' you are literally sending elements and forces ahead of your body that will arrange things to make your visit or journey pleasant. When before the visit or the journey or the shopping trip you are in a bad humour, or fearful or apprehensive of something unpleasant, you are sending unseen agencies ahead of you which will make some kind of unpleasantness. Our thoughts, or in other words, our state of mind, is ever at work 'fixing up' things good or bad in advance.* "

PRENTICE MULFORD

" Everything you can imagine is real."

PABLO PICASSO

*" Our thought is the unseen magnet,
ever attracting its correspondence
in things seen and tangible."*

PRENTICE MULFORD

But what if my manifesting goes against my destiny?

We are all familiar with the idea of 'what will be will be,' the notion that our destiny is already decided. How can there be a place for manifesting if our destiny is already sewn up? It is helpful to understand the difference between our 'fate' and our 'destiny', or 'providence'. Our 'fate', the ancients believed, is what will happen to us if we merely fall back on our base, animal instincts. If we don't put any effort in to our lives, we will suffer our 'fate'. Our destiny or providence, on the other hand, is what awaits us if we listen to the divine and embrace our human potential. Manifesting is therefore an alignment of our potential with our divine destiny.

Meet Thomas Troward, an English legislator who worked in 19th-century India. He synthesized Western and Eastern philosophy and is credited in the 2006 film *The Secret* with being one of the founding fathers of the 'Laws of Attraction Philosophy'. He delivered a series of lectures in 1904 examining the power of our mind and the 'universal mind' to manifest desired outcomes.

" By thus making intelligent use of our subjective mind, we, so to speak, create a nucleus, which is no sooner created than it begins to exercise an attractive force, drawing to itself material of a like character with its own, and if this process is allowed to go on undisturbed, it will continue until an external form corresponding to the nature of the nucleus comes out into manifesting on the plane of the objective and relative."

THOMAS TROWARD

"Desire. . . will in due time externalize itself as concrete fact."

THOMAS TROWARD

"*Everyone is made of matter, and matter is continually going through a chemical change. This change is life, not wisdom, but life, like vegetable or mineral life. Every idea is matter, so of course it contains life in the name of something that can be changed. Motion, or change, is life. Ideas have life. A belief has life, or matter; for it can be changed.*"

PHINEUS QUIMBY

Gratitude is the sister of manifesting. The ability to notice and express gratitude over small pleasures, small rewards and small kindnesses will allow you to reap great rewards later.

" The thankful heart will find, in every hour, some heavenly blessings."

HENRY WARD BEECHER

" *Use the imagination to picture only what is good, what is beautiful, what is beneficial, what is ideal, and what you wish to realize. Mentally see yourself receiving what you deeply desire to receive. What you imagine, you will think, and what you think, you will become. Therefore, if you imagine only those things that are in harmony with what you wish to obtain or achieve, all your thinking will soon tend to produce what you want to attain or achieve.* "

CHRISTIAN D. LARSON

The art of manifesting has been recognized and utilized by some of history's finest minds.

Meet Nikola Tesla, the Serbian-born American physicist who visualized and manifested his own inventions. His work contributed to the remote control, wireless technology, neon lights, hydroelectric power and most usefully the alternate current (AC) – the basis for our present-day electric system. Thank goodness he dived into his own imagination and fantasies to create world-enhancing inventions.

" In my boyhood I suffered from a peculiar affliction due to the appearance of images, often accompanied by strong flashes of light ... These were at first very blurred and indistinct... but by and by I succeeded in fixing them; they gained in strength and distinctness and finally assumed the concreteness of real things. Every night (and sometimes during the day), when alone, I would start on my journeys — see new places, cities and countries — live there, meet people and make friendships and acquaintances and, however unbelievable, it is a fact that they were just as dear to me as those in actual life and not a bit less

*intense in their manifestings... This
I did constantly until I was about
seventeen when my thoughts turned
seriously to invention. Then I observed
to my delight that I could visualize
with the greatest facility. I needed no
models, drawings or experiments. I
could picture them all as real in my
mind."*

NIKOLA TESLA

Imagine the scene. It's 1896 and the then world's most famous actress Sarah Bernhardt hosts a party and introduces inventor and manifestor Nikola Tesla to Indian yogi Swami Vivekananda. They discuss *prâna* (energy), *âkâsha* (matter) and *kalpas* (time). A friendship develops and they share ideas of universal energy and the potential synthesis of Western and Eastern cosmology. In this vivid whirl of mathematics and meditation, energy and electricity, ideas of manifesting as we now understand it found their modern foundations.

" The day science begins to study non-physical phenomena, it will make more progress in one decade than in all the previous centuries of its existence. If you want to find the secrets of the universe, think in terms of energy, frequency and vibration."

NIKOLA TESLA

Imagine like a child

Children are blessed with undisciplined, vivid and often entirely bonkers imaginations. You can picture it now: the toddler who says they want to be a tomato when they grow up, or the child who wishes to marry their bunny rabbit. As we age, our hopes and dreams become more ordered and realistic but less instinctive and vivid. When you're next manifesting, try to recapture your untethered childhood imagination.

How to manifest like a child

Set no limits on where your imagination can take you. If you are working towards a new house, for example, and picture yourself perched atop a rainbow, allow yourself to stay there and meditate on what this may mean. A new horizon? A new journey? No house at all, but a bridge elsewhere?

Be as silly as possible. You need to open more income streams, surely this is no time for silliness? Wrong. Be creative in your thinking.

What first appears in your mind as a clown's costume could manifest into a successful fancy-dress costume business.

Be in the present. Children demand immediate love, care and attention. Give these to yourself in your manifesting requests.

" Imagination is the beginning of creation. You imagine what you desire, and will what you imagine, and at last you create what you will."

GEORGE BERNARD SHAW

Far from being a solitary activity seeking only to achieve for oneself, manifesting has the power to be a generous endeavour with the potential to benefit others. If you can be as enthusiastic about the success of others as about the success of yourself, you will send such momentous blasts of positive energy out into the cosmos that it will invariably shower down on you in return.

Manifest for others

1. When manifesting for yourself, send positive vibes out to someone you know who could also benefit from what you are seeking.

2. Invite friends to manifest with you.

3. Understand that every time you support others' journeys, you allow positive energy to continue its forward momentum.

4. Celebrate enthusiastically when a friend's manifesting is successful, even if yours hasn't yet come to fruition.

Create a 'face board' of the attribute you wish to embody

For example, if you wish to become more courageous, meditating on the images of those well-known for embodying bravery can help. Assemble a mood board of instantly recognizable figures whose courage speaks personally to you. Select members of your own family, fictional characters and thought leaders from history and contemporary society. Placing Harry Potter alongside Martin Luther King and Great Aunt Peggy next to Joan of Arc will remind you that courage can be summoned in everyone, including you.

"When an object or purpose is clearly held in thought, its precipitation, in tangible and visible form, is merely a question of time. The vision always precedes, and itself determines the realization."

LILIAN WHITING

Approach manifesting with enthusiasm and energy. The energy you are able to devote to your desire will propel it towards fruition. American poet Lilian Whiting wrote passionately about the importance of enthusiasm when approaching life's challenges.

"No one has success until he has the abounding life. This is made up of the many-fold activity of energy, enthusiasm and gladness. It is to spring to meet the day with a thrill at being alive. It is to go forth to meet the morning in an ecstasy of joy. It is to realize the oneness of humanity."

LILIAN WHITING

How to continue manifesting when success isn't being immediately achieved

1. Consider if your goals need editing to become more specific.

2. Circle back to your original intention and jot down ways you have attempted to follow through – is there more you could do?

3. Shake up your manifesting method. If you manifest in bed at night with candles and essential oils, try sharing your desires outside while forest bathing.

4. Trust in the cosmos, and find peace in the patience of waiting for your desire to be made manifest in its own good time.

Manifesting looks like. . .

Fantasizing

Forward planning

Harnessing energy

Imagining

Being intentional

" To every man there openeth
A Way, and Ways, and a Way.
And the High Soul climbs the High Way,
And the Low Soul gropes the Low,
And in between, on the misty flats,
The rest drift to and fro.
But to every man there openeth
A High Way, and a Low.
And every man decideth
The Way his soul shall go."

JOHN OXENHAM

Manifesting impresses upon us that we are all connected to the universe, so be alive and observant to the opportunities roundabout. Watch! Observe! Notice! Take note! Listen! Tune in! By keeping an open-hearted observation on the world all around, you will be receptive to words, opportunities and openings. When you catch glimpses of these golden chances, act!

Remember that you would not have been given longings without the capacity and abilities to fulfil them.

" I desire
And I crave"

SAPPHO

Sappho was a Greek poet (from whose name the word 'sapphic' is derived), and her fragmentary poems are some of the earliest recorded inward desires of a woman. She was looking up from her ordinary existence and longing for something more.

Adopt Sappho's poetry for your own manifesting chants:

I *desire*
And I *crave*...
... a home of my own.

I *desire*
And I *crave*...
... a partner who loves as I love.

I *desire*
And I *crave*...
... riches to bestow wisely.

Practise close reading your affirmations and intentions

We easily fall into the habit of glancing, scanning and scrolling through text. We lightly skim over the words, forgetting them as our attention is drawn to the next thing. Where manifesting affirmations are concerned, each word needs to be savoured, repeated and deeply understood.

Contemplate each word and meditate on its significance to understand what your affirmation truly means and requires of you.

I am a source of joy to my family.

I: my body and my soul, my actions, my words and my thoughts.

Am: my being, now, in this moment.

A source: a fountainhead, a giver.

Of joy: happiness, laughter, wellbeing, pleasure.

To my family: him, her, them, my people, individuals bound by love.

Five-second manifesting idea

Say your weekly intention out loud. That's it. Don't be embarrassed – be bold in your intention.

'I am increasing in prosperity.'

Five-second manifesting idea

Whisper your daily intention to yourself three times.

'I am kind to everyone I meet.'

'I am kind to everyone I meet.'

'I am kind to everyone I meet.'

Five-second manifesting idea

Step outside, close your eyes and turn your face to the sun. Send your conscious desire to our closest star.

'I am healthy, strong and I am open to the energy of the cosmos.'

Five-second manifesting idea

Tell one person what you are manifesting today. Begin by saying you have something you wish to share with them. Reveal your manifesting intention and thank them for being part of your journey.

'I deserve a lover who cares for me with as much loving kindness as I do.'

What is creativity if not the act of manifesting an emotion into a painting, a piece of music, a poem, a clay pot, a perfect pudding? Artists, inventors and composers throughout history have described this almost ineffable business of crafting a feeling into something tangible. From the child who makes a mud pie to Michaelangelo coaxing statues from stone, all humans have an unlimited capacity to create objects from ideas. Give yourself permission and space to allow creativity to manifest itself in your life.

Genius composers Beethoven and Mozart described the electrifying acts of creativity whereby music appeared almost perfectly formed in their minds, simply requiring them to harness and transcribe the details. These acts of musical manifesting bear witness to the awe-inspiring power of human creativity.

"You ask me where I get my ideas.
That I cannot tell you with certainty.
They come unsummoned, directly,
indirectly – I could seize them with
my hands – out in the open air, in the
woods, while walking, in the silence of
the nights, at dawn, excited by moods
which are translated by the poet into
words, by me into tones that sound and
roar and storm about me till I have set
them down in notes."

LUDWIG VAN BEETHOVEN

" The whole, though it be long, stands almost complete and finished in my mind so that I can survey it at a glance. Nor do I hear in my imagination the parts successively, but I hear them, as it were, all at once. What delight this is I cannot tell!"

WOLFGANG AMADEUS MOZART

"Focus more on your desire than on your doubt, and the dream will take care of itself."

MARK TWAIN

"I was in darkness, but I took three steps and found myself in paradise. The first step was a good thought, the second, a good word; and the third, a good deed."

FREIDRICH NIETZSCHE

Practise the total absorption manifesting technique to unblock a stubborn manifestation

You have shared your intention with the cosmos: 'My relationship with my mother is repaired', for example. The intention is firmly lodged in your subconscious. You have been at peace with the intention for some time but your intention has not manifested into reality. Now is the time to embrace the total absorption technique.

1. Choose an activity that will allow you to become entirely absorbed in its completion: redecorating the spare room, icing a cake, walking in the woods.

2. Before you begin, repeat your intention: 'My relationship with my

mother is healthy and repaired'. Do not ruminate on it: put it from your mind and begin the task at hand.

3. Allow yourself to become totally absorbed in your work. Notice all the sensory responses provoked – the crunch of the woodland floor or the smell of the cake.

4. While the mind is occupied elsewhere, space is made for inspiration to arrive and your intention to manifest as an idea.

5. Listen to what arrives in your mind. A whisper of a thought for reconciliation. Perhaps the cosmos will have suggested you take the cake to your mother, invite her to walk in the woods or view the new room.

"Nature, like a kind and smiling mother, lends herself to our dreams and cherishes our fancies."

VICTOR HUGO

It can be helpful to calibrate your manifesting style to suit your mindset type. If you are unsure what your mindset type is, think carefully about how you process and approach situations in life and ask friends how they view you.

Mindset type

1. Problem-solving mindset
2. Romantic mindset
3. Fear mindset
4. Intuitive mindset

Manifesting method suggestion

1. Methodical manifesting journaling
2. Narrative manifesting scripting
3. Manifesting with a friend to share your concerns
4. Outdoor manifesting, under the stars or in woodland

"That is the principal thing – not to remain with the dream, with the intention, with the being-in-the-mood, but always forcibly to convert it all into things."

RAINER MARIA RILKE

For as long as people have slept, they have placed charms, wishes and intentions beneath their pillows. During the Song Dynasty in China, men would sleep on ceramic pillows carved into the shapes of beautiful women to summon such visions in their sleep. In English folklore, 'groaning cakes' were placed under unmarried women's pillows with the hope that their future love would appear to them as they slept. In Romania on 6th January, girls would place sprigs of basil beneath their pillows for a vision of their future love.

How to use the pillow method of manifesting

1. Write your desire on a piece of paper that won't hinder your sleep.

2. If you wish to incorporate a special number, then copy your intention out your chosen number of times.

3. Open a window and read your intention aloud into the night sky. Direct your intention to a star or planet that has particular meaning, or the cosmos at large.

4. Kiss your piece of paper (because kisses always help).

5. Place beneath your pillow.

6. As you prepare your mind and body for sleep, repeat your intention a chosen number of times or until you slide into sleep.

7. Sleep peacefully, knowing that as you rest, your intention is seeping into your subconscious.

8. Repeat with a fresh piece of paper each night for a week.

Three ways to enhance the pillow manifesting method

1. Anoint your intention with an essential oil that has a particular resonance either with you or your desire, such as lavender for relaxation, lemon for invigoration, patchouli for sensuality or neroli for joy.

2. Accompany your intention with a note of gratitude to the cosmos. Write, 'I thank you for my manifold gifts and good fortune.'

3. Note down your dreams the morning after your pillow manifesting and consider if the cosmos is already responding to your intention.

"Imagine for yourself a character, a model personality, whose example you determine to follow, in private as well as in public."

EPICTETUS

Utilize the language of crystals to support your manifesting journey. Either place these beneath your pillow with your notes of intention and affirmation or close by in your favourite manifesting space.

Rose quartz and rhodonite for love.

Citrine and pyrite for wealth.

Garnet and bloodstone for health.

Carnelian for creativity.

Green jade and aventurine for success.

Bookend your day with manifesting

By crafting your manifesting rituals around the beginning and end of your day, you create a powerful balance to your manifesting. Try a strong intention in the morning and then a thoughtful reflection and rebooted manifesting in the evening. Create rituals that complement your daily life and can be viewed with pleasure rather than reluctance. Don't make them so lengthy that there isn't time to shower, or so brief that you haven't fully absorbed the intention.

Morning manifesting rituals

Spend two minutes standing in front of an open window. Speak your intention aloud to the morning sky.

Chant your manifesting intention your chosen number of times in the shower.

Drink your coffee in complete stillness, concentrating only on your intention.

Place your manifesting vision board in the kitchen. Ignore your phone and look only at the board while you eat.

Script your manifesting intentions before putting on makeup. As you apply each product, imagine you are daubing your intentions into your being.

Evening manifesting rituals

Keep track of sunset and at the fall of darkness say, 'I place my intentions in the care of the night.'

As you remove your makeup and cleanse yourself from the day, visualize yourself removing doubt and negativity in preparation for a new day.

Spend two minutes standing in front of an open window. Speak your intention into the night sky.

Instead of using electronic devices before bed, rescript the morning's intention to place beneath your pillow.

While awaiting sleep, silently chant your intention as you would count sheep, drifting to sleep on the waves of your words.

Ten night-time mantras

I thank this day for its gifts, both wanted and unwanted.

I turn into the night to sleep and place my faith in the abundant cosmos.

I am embracing the journey and send my vision to the care of the night.

The day has ended, the night is drawing in, my journey continues.

I sleep bathed in the bounty of the universe.

As I repeat my intentions, I understand that an unseen energy supports me.

I will succeed. I will succeed. I
will succeed.

As I drift into sleep, my dream gathers
energy until I am ready to meet it.

My intentions will grow stronger with
the passage of the night.

I will wake rested, with my vision
burning bright.

QUOTES ARE TAKEN FROM

Charles F. Haanel, 1866–1949, American businessman and philosopher

Christian D. Larson, 1874–1962, American New Thought leader

Emily Dickinson, 1830–1886, American poet and recluse

Epictetus, c. AD 50–135, former slave and Stoic philosopher

Erwin Schrödinger, 1887–1961, Nobel Prize-winning Austrian physicist

Friedrich Nietzsche, 1844–1900, German philosopher

George Augustus Sala, 1828–1895, English journalist

George Bernard Shaw, 1856–1950, Irish playwright

Giordano Bruno, 1548–1600, Italian cosmological theorist

Henry Ward Beecher, 1813–1887, American clergyman and social reformer

Herbert Kaufman, 1878–1947, American journalist

John Oxenham, 1852–1941, English poet and hymn writer

Lilian Whiting, 1847–1942, American writer

Ludwig van Beethoven, 1770–1827, German composer

Mark Twain, 1835–1910 American writer

Max Planck, 1858–1947, Nobel Prize-winning discoverer of energy quanta

Nathaniel Hawthorne, 1804–1864, American author

Nikola Tesla, 1856–1943, Serbian-American inventor

Novalis, 1772–1801, German polymath and poet

Pablo Picasso, 1881–1973, Spanish artist

Phineas Quimby, 1802–1866, American founder of New Thought spiritual movement

Pliny the Elder, c. AD 23–79, Roman natural philosopher

Plotinus, c. AD 205–270, Hellenistic metaphysical philosopher

Prentice Mulford, 1834–1891, American author

Rainer Maria Rilke, 1875–1926, Austrian writer

Ralph Waldo Emerson, 1803–1882, American philosopher and essayist

Sappho, 625–570 BC, Greek lyric poet

Thales, c. 624–c. 546 BC, Greek philosopher

Thomas Troward, 1847–1916, English author

Victor Hugo, 1802–1885, French author

Winston Churchill, 1874–1965, British prime minister and statesman

Wolfgang Amadeus Mozart, 1756–1791, Austrian composer

BIBLIOGRAPHY AND
FURTHER READING

The Secret, Rhonda Byrne, Simon & Schuster, 2006

The Law of Attraction, Esther and Jerry Hicks, Hay House 2006

Manifest: 7 Steps to Living Your Best Life, Roxie Nafousi, Michael Joseph, 2022

The Master Key System, Charles F. Haanel, republished by Wilder Publications, 2022

The Life Radiant, Lilian Whiting, republished by CreateSpace, 2012

USEFUL WEBSITES

berkeleywellbeing.com

manifestationbabe.com

mindbodygreen.com

oprahdaily.com

thelawofattraction.com

roxienafousi.com

Managing Director Sarah Lavelle
Assistant Editor Sofie Shearman
Words Joanna Gray
Series Designer Emily Lapworth
Designer Katy Everett
Head of Production Stephen Lang
Production Controller Martina Georgieva

Published in 2023 by Quadrille,
an imprint of Hardie Grant
Publishing

Quadrille
52–54 Southwark Street
London SE1 1UN
quadrille.com

The publisher has made every
effort to trace the copyright
holders. We apologize in advance
for any unintentional omissions
and would be pleased to insert the
appropriate acknowledgement in
any subsequent edition.

Cataloguing in Publication Data:
a catalogue record for this book is
available from the British Library.

ISBN 978 1 83783 050 3

Printed in China

MIX
Paper | Supporting
responsible forestry
FSC™ C020056
FSC
www.fsc.org